Etruria

Wave Books Seattle/New York

Rodney Koeneke

Published by Wave Books

www.wavepoetry.com

Copyright © 2014 by Rodney Koeneke

Wave Books titles are distributed to the trade by

Consortium Book Sales and Distribution

Phone: 800–283–3572 / SAN 631–760X

Library of Congress Cataloging–in–Publication Data

Koeneke, Rodney.

[Poems. Selection]

Etruria / Rodney Koeneke. — First Edition.

pages cm

ISBN 978–1–933517–82–7 (limited edition hardcover: alk. paper)

ISBN 978–1–933517–81–0 (trade pbk.: alk. paper)

I. Title.

PS3611.O363E89 2013

813'.6—dc23

2013017486

Designed and composed by Quemadura

Printed in the United States of America

9 8 7 6 5 4 3 2 1

First Edition

Wave Books 040

for

LESLEY POIRIER

(1966–2011)

und wir saßen beieinander

Far more probably, the city itself lay on that opposite hill there, which lies splendid and unsullied, running parallel to us. —D. H. Lawrence, *Etruscan Places*

Etruria

Toward a Theory of Translation

Everyone knows that O'Hara is great, but who loses much sleep over

Pasternak?

In Russia, where the poem is still valued

as a succession of more or less beautiful lines, creation

is also regarded as the province of the Devil. Life and its regulation

belong to dumb forces, which collect at a shining point the green

translator would probably

render as God, while spontaneity erupts (to borrow a favorite Russian

image) like a fish

breaking out from the ice, flopping from the water to thrash and heave

in air.

Somewhere in this passage I'm certain it suffers a kind of epiphany,

which is often celebrated in poems but elsewhere finds itself less

welcome,

even despised. The motifs most common to Russian poetry (it's

perhaps useful here to

consider "text" as something woven, like underwear or rugs) are rich

but few: a monk

converses with his starets, or elder; features of the landscape such as

ponds, clouds, and

weather are addressed familiarly by the poet; a mule or duck suddenly

speaks

to its owner, describing in tears the heretofore unconsidered

awkwardness of its servitude.

1

Each exchange bears its measure of pathos, like women in the
   Caucasus with baskets
balanced squarely on their heads, but it leaves little room for that boozy
   sprezzatura
O'Hara or a dozen other poets achieved midcentury on a 40-block
   stretch of Manhattan.

All this is by way of saying that if love is a state for which no language
   is ever adequate,
yet we keep falling in love and writing about it anyway, then each of us,
in our private feelings, resembles a poem waiting for its translator, like
   a lover
who waits for a lover on the steps of a bank or somewhere municipal,
   knowing how pale
and approximate any discussion of feelings will finally be, despite the
   original's
undeniable power. The nonsensical, or phatic—defined by Jakobson as
   that which lifts the
fish through the ice, then gives it nothing to breathe—has perhaps been
   too little esteemed
in translation, or anywhere else; for though I am no O'Hara, just being
   with you I manage
to feel elevated, a trainful of Russians passing over Manhattan, happy
   to gesture or shout or
merely gasp.

The Real Aeneid

Then went down with the ships

then taught at community colleges

taught greek

was talking, teaching, was teaching the boys with eyes closed

talking, then America moved beneath me

professors, goodbye

keep in your place while the nation moves

the urban will be visited on rail towns

the rural debouch into office jobs

rising in glamour above a large city

the rich and the young are anxious to get drunk in

each winking as if she were happy

and happiness a system

and buildings were its dwelling

and winkingness its sign.

Then remembered a feeling of dissolving

which temporarily left this image in my mind:

Pringles, Pringles on everything, fresh junk

soiling autumn's reggae

sloe-eyed children breathing gin

syntax moving in fingery legions

expiring like Lazarus, Lazarus, get up

history's ashes a TV series

the peasantry snoring unevenly through it

time's smeared uneven dream

Dissolved in a system

that reconstituted me as tears

it's like I was dead, it was glory

sat next to the ships

inside a fresh body

tears, a great presence of eyes

I didn't care what theory taught

I was the greeny excrescence

of everything theory wanted,

crystal scooped from the centers of things

as if for the singing world to come into

as if things could speak, and I taught them

torn by them and the creatures that dance for them

and knew it, knew the timeless

numbed in the zero—

Dido, it's me, I'm not hungry

Dido, don't cry, it's just sleep.

Billet-don't

You and your schoolmarm grammar. Me and my fake Greek.

To court me in this language of a Finnish peasant fucked improperly

at the equinox: *Mieleni Minun Tekevi*—I am driven

by my longing, languid as East Kansas, my teeth grown soft

like Chiclets, sad casualties of night.

Moon, I think you're cooling. Dreams get more terse, your

exegeses of them obscurer and, on the coast where misprision

swats at foam, each word deliquesces with morning

into its opposite—"Come hithers" to "*Vale, fratres*," "Venetian"

to "Venusian," logic to lyric, cherry to choke.

Dinosaurs escape the barns of slumber

and slither into the remoter villages of my feelings

to join its dark stories: brother consumes sister, sister

marries father, crone boils babies, druids bone crones

and niceties like plot and conclusion and bourgeois time

Are as out of place as ostriches in a Finnish national epic,

or scruples in our hot friendship, or snowmen half-assembled

on the lawns of spring's pavilions, where everything cold is exposed

as excuses for melting, then quicklime for burning

Then rugs for your Cossack boots. My Sibyl of leaves

and longing, I was once of sane mind

and stallions used to pull me drunk through evening.

Now just closing eyes takes a giant effort

and I am a sleepless fan of nearly everything you do.

Tristia

Go, little book, to her, where I can't enter
and serve as her doorjamb, or bookshelf prop, or coaster
or a clean spot on the floor for her to drop

her T-shirts or negligee (forbidden!), or be that place
where she can indolently tuck her billets-doux
that accumulate, and she pushes them aside irresponsibly

to look at maybe when she gets moderately loaded
on warm fall evenings. Suggest to her then
the advantages of having done with being a lover

and the small claim that entails on the other's attention—
how you become the other of an other, how corners
grow eyes, phone calls smart, one minute you burn, the next

you're gelatinous as cold spaghetti. She is young
and subject to crushes; go, pervy book, and say how often
her breasts crush against the bodies of newish lovers,

place my lines in her ears at moments of passion
like children's prayers simulating Formica—bright little desires
stuck to a matrix in which they're entirely foreign—

and inflect her basically ardent, genteel nature
with a careful pity for my situation
where phenomena struggle but I'm not allowed to answer,

but want to, then can't, then feel empty

as a disused sports center. Then be convivial, speak casually

and tell how the vocative is a legitimate grammatical function,

how she should call, or call out, and perhaps one time I'll come over

to analyze her poems or something equally unsexy, cerebral.

Remind her that words are Persians, freeing Hebrews

while baiting Greeks, and that what a lover says to

a lover (anywhere, at any time) is written on wind,

on water. Be talisman of my absent glamour, a pretty synecdoche

for me. Don't tell how I comport myself at orgies

with the stateliness of a dowager, how frequently in love I resemble

a lapsed blog or a model train enthusiast. Speak if you have to just

nonsense

to prolong communication, be of ice trays and weather

or kitchen implements, minutiae seldom thought of as romantic

but in a song this slender

enough to keep it from ending,

delaying that point where I have to go home and remember

she's there, I'm here, deep in Thai donut

shop radio stutter, reminding the crullers

of *carmen et error*, the dull irk of distance,

how gorgeous she made even loam.

sharon mesmer

Sharon get up

be cinema again

for long pearly stretches the sky isn't anything

but stars

inside the theaters

projectors push light through emulsions

soon we'll be peasants

films digitally perfect

sugars beat by threshers from the cane

with alarming new efficiency

mixed in low-calorie sodas

and presented to you at your table

as if it were 16, blond you

behind the stockyards

enduring the matinee of being Polish

eyes & a moon & silence

rivers outside the theaters

filling with evening's cerise

there isn't a syntax

to carry its light

light isn't syntax

it just holds everything.

Tiny Spark

Days in obedience, love as form

in daughters bringing cans to empty churches

here I am ejecting grayscale subjects

creating cross-racial primary care relations in a nurse

because we lived inside a shtetl

all caregivers knew what would happen

regular dental obedience

in culturally mixed careerist/parent dyads

some people think without logos

or without that little spark some people have

a worker in vapory Singapore

packs labor into sound

names of flags suggest themselves

to work all forty American mother-child combos

I judge them via earbud

in my spare time, as I sleep

rinsed cash silent

on shelves in basement jars

I am aware of my little spark

I am of my little spark proud

abbreviated clouds

wet summer monetizers

cruise the asymmetry

of me to Iranian world sound

in crepuscule to someone

without old dreams but forms

the old dreams take

Ossians policing contradictions——

I love my little spark because it's mine

chinoiserie

Meet me at the autumn gate
where trees collect to skin the imperial
lake with discharged verdure. Everything Kenny dismisses
is actually interesting: you will see the ducts
as we continue to walk a little,
    this month of quiet weather
subtracting the thorns from the rose.

Look where the willows thread their fingers
through dust outside the gate:
all ceremony of motion has stopped
    the traffic stilled
moons distribute coins indifferently
to the poor and lightless hushed against the walls
pretending to autumns
officials don't feel

Except sometimes in willows.
Come to the Gate of Autumn
I am distracted and Kenny dismissed
everything anyone dismisses is actually interesting
    oak released from forest,
willows moved back from the road.

Dawn touches the butte, we are leaving.
Cold orb, where I think to find the way,

                        say no.

I Should Feel Happy

I should feel happy, but I can't.
Life is an uneven way—cranes
flap over the mountain tarn,
dew condenses on the lichens:
very overwhelming!
Sitting on a cloud or hill
covered by other clouds, watching the cranes
form into a vee beneath me:
When will I know? How will I know it?
I have the most awesome friends ever,
I am not happy at all.
Tears cover my face, drown my heart
why can't you write English
like a song that is played over radio
and makes me hurt inside?
I hate my roommate, don't have any money
my plans are easy but won't come down smoothly
through the wet arcades of the firs.
I am a little afraid
of what it will feel like
when she isn't here and I am alone
with musicians who will overstay their welcome.
By the time we're there
you, too, will be weary
of my eloquence, the easy rapture
I once got from your eyes

will dissipate into bulbous clouds

over the midday sky, it overcast

and the musicians continuing to sing.

I am not happy alone with the cranes

I drink to assure many people

of the light in the tavern of your eyes

I drink to assure them

its mild intoxication

was simple because of your eyes.

I Am Sitting in a Room

I am sitting in a room, recording
within the relatively narrow radius of life.
Inside of time, what happens is a business
for bringing my heart to sick.
Events are like a measure of its fullness.
They accrete in time, my heart gets sick,
a dog come through the redwoods with a bluebird
partly moving at the edges,
stiff where it once was soft.

Or else I'll be sitting here reading,
"To write of the bird
or the bulldozer atop it?"
my heart in that moment
a chieftain's new helmet
decorated with repetitions
against life's extra hazards
which is after all just part of the human outlook, right?

And I find if I'm gone
I am not alone in leaving
recording from this room, now here
now imagining you
here with me, not reading
yet standing near competing with the chorus

warmed in the open wings

susceptible as August, its

degrees at record heat

And I completely stop recording

for a while while taking showers together

with you in science and compassion

being brought back into presence

against a really attractive template,

contingency a glistering

filament over night.

Perhaps it is perfection in the life

- that cancels the whole output being created right now;

we press time under Lucite,

send e-mails with no subject

linking others to a business

that rests a banner in completion never

knowing how far and difficult

this process of emergence

will again and again try to be.

Still you remain positive

regarding it as a kind of narrative

going serenely in one direction

through the major life blows

then saying when the brook

asks the mill-boss of his daughter,

"If this badly I still love her

after pushing at your labor

I, too, want to remain positive.

Do you have any advice for me?"

ghazal

pyaara, you can't tell you need me badly
so I'll tell the meanings of some words first

ahh is a sign for the poet's crying
beneath it your sighs push open the throat's lost doors

who lives alone to wish for your lengths of *zulf*
is one who won't live long to wish alone

halqa's a ring, *sad* means hundred
misshapen bumps convened on a massy pearl

this poem is a solitary circle
the world is sad a hundred different ways

heart, build up your fire like a neighbor
getting too drunk at spring's first barbecue

how quick are the pure to repulse the despised
how slowly those nipples would answer my caress

think what small change the water has to suffer
to be itself and several different drops

the bee that's come to love its sweet partitions
the body in the cupfuls of its cells

I will fold up my health like a garment

for you to forget in the ebony groove of your chest

the afterparty after the afterparty

and after afterparties?

god for how long will remain a flaneur

in his own café on his own boulevard?

now boss, don't take what's said above for granted

its surface was the parts I understand

the bed conceals its lexicon of stones

but scows above still find the river fluent

I write for the people, my feelings were simple

it's readers make a complicated hell

the words themselves deflect my depth of meaning

I think you don't know yet how long I can sit at your door

could someone give this *sher* its right translation?

the liar who writes it lies right before my eyes

Rodney, no translation is ever satisfactory—

be foreign only to its disappointments

Pyjamas

To me she is in her pyjamas
Crusaders brought from Persia
   to dress up the ladies
they weren't to touch

Look what I brought you
these ampules of feeling
women who sing in the cold hall at the cressets,
   sing with me

Me in the cotton with my halberd
you in your wardrobe at prayers
Sky with its feeling of entourage
for those who don't move with the night

Lover, does it matter
how the river spends its glitter,
where the freighter leaves its sugar
as it swings through the low mountain towns?

Look what it brought you—
these wedding knives in velvet
they fit you like nightclothes
   made of others' labor,

Children twisting wire

for the diadems you wear.

    Why is it the lesser

never you think will have power?

The thinking of the loving

    is the loving

the ankle sings most sweetly

        in its sock

I do not plan to die

like the feminine pronoun

I have pulled up my socks again and again for you

I will pull them and stand here and sing

Occitan Reverb

The leaf swings: I don't hold it
it's on to other subjects
once new, now pushed by low sighs
whose melodies are easy
I see them move in bitter air
though sweet in place and season
its leaves
that soon will prosper
the bad will be over
the sweet will enter my heart
it will be sweet there
in turn for each pain

Noises for the Talkies

I don't know

the book enacts a tension

performativity's brushed

wars discussed

there's ways of reading

everything wars erect

as fodder for considering

my pain inside the poem

assume for a minute a product

soon a country's attached

a soldier, a leg

the pendulum, when it swings

a hired operative tired almost of itself

like the unit it's a part of

closing the stops that reify

       the poem,

its box of loose breath

I invoke as I shelter

a stranger here, an anti-god

resplendent with meaning

it sings but it can't go back to

I don't know

it sings

but it can't go back

The Women Are Weaning at the Cutter of the Now

The women should by now be employed in preparing roots for the cutter

when the wether lambs were in fashion

they came right up the back door

at the call of the brethren

we have such high notions

when there is not a leaf on this tree we sit and swing

and sing

it is in the character of the weaned

to be as we are now

at the pressure of the constant

the plants should be straining to set roots to the new

one could measure out land as needed

humidity in unheated rooms

their roots will begin to go deeper for more water

we have short time for cutting

but now the recovered

where troubles were intended

by the Author said the brethren

to wean us from fondness for life.

nichita stănescu

Who am I?

Nothing.

Who is Nothing?

A poet.

stănescu is said
to have removed the hinges
from his door

so he could drink more honorably
with his fellow citizens.

Community Sing

It remembers the acrid fumes

it waits in the creases

of something forgotten we've forgotten we're not

supposed to be doing, I mean why

do they work, these verbs

on the radio's dreaming, I mean

to be a narwhal just once for sublimity

the most socially awkward demographic of the ocean community

synapses spinning like Greek plates:

you can do the same thing to consciousness

with words. Can it be like a moustache?

That atrophies with use?

A community moustache

left in a drawer, then just when you expect

that its function is to be decorative

suddenly you pat your lip and something there,

it's grown?

I have seen fear in a community housing forum

I fly the glum skyway, I circle, I freeze.

How can we speak about empathy

beneath the lonely curl of menthol

that is Jane Bowles?

What makes us this unpopular

at the volunteer student raffles

this dimness in walkways, this blot in the skyway,

this particular gumbo, these trees?

"You can come clean in a dirty place" (LRSN)

created for you when you joined the community

or you can pretend not to recognize

the sharp smells coming up from the river

transparently aimed at pleasing internationals

statements that smell of profit and incinerator

the scorched poor hugging the base of the mountain

singing in assembly

look there it is it's community

it remembers

it remembers still

it still remembers what we were supposed to be doing

it remembers what we feel like if it leaves.

Indignant Puppies

Teach the puppies bite inhibition

then act all indignant

and teach that no business should look to their flattened ears

We teach them they need to hurt humans if the need arises

here is your need

it's a screenshot of me chucking puppies off cliffs

now you will claim to be indignant and promise to investigate

Red heart, come back from your slumber

Once it is fallen, I will assess its condition

I want to stay angry and indignant so that I can also stay

open and alive

valerie bertinelli

I am a girl who sees the world in everything.
I wonder in a 100 years if the world will just flip.
I upload the roar of children, chop cauliflower
because I want to see the ones I love
as loving me forever. I see colorful daisies
as the children of lawns
swaying unfruitfully in the wind. I want the ones
who pretend they are without wings to protect me
touch sun, feel hearts—
in that instant I understand almost everything

Pretending I am flying
over the worry and loss of this city
into the warm sun, to touch who I can.
I worry, making canapés over the sink,
that nothing will be easy, ever
if all of this is happening for reasons,
that that family is my family, crying out in pain,
thin daisies bent flat in a summer wind.

I understand that almost, when they cry
why nothing is easy in this world with its reasons.
I pretend I am without wings to protect me—
I dream one day of a city that's at peace.
I see something good that is in everyone. In a 100
years I wonder will the world just flip.

Googly World

It's a Googly world now. The rise of an empire continues

technology its leader, but in the undercarriage a behemoth

consults to the young via agencies

for eating your own googly eyes.

In this fast-moving world we all sometimes ignore the moving view

too quickly—kids making poems

onto tea bags they send out to world leaders

you view some of the facts they've inserted there on the tea

the world leader drinks it

See, these are ideas we can license to others

to experience feelings of confidence and safety

as curators continue to glue googly eyes

onto D.C. rebellion leaders

then post them to Flickr

in the United States, or anywhere else

that has more money than Caligula

to get points across with

While we, with our new baby

products, what happens

if we license to others

this incredible daffodil scent?

Happy Xmas

Why encumber the reindeer with Santa?

Whereas from a global standpoint distance drives costs polar.

Data suggesting warming, gifts insubstantial,

the managers typically they manage the business from a great distance.

All foreign entrants are equally illegal;

we can help them plot the surface we can't help them

make it home. If you would like to "guesstimate" a distance,

we can help to plot the surface

but time constraints encumber work.

We had just enough time to get clear of the water tower

and it's hard to think of work.

Revered like a Santa in China

but manufactured somewhere else, because of cost of Fibre.

Language of resistance,

or quitters who refuse to go the distance?

We simplify the problems by approximation,

examine each problem with at least three different solutions.

Foreign institutions with the right to encumber your credit—

that hurts the other networks' network business.

Too many of these amendments start to look bad for fibre.

We have lots of the same data, we can work

to plot the distance, but why encumber santa

with foreigners of this caliber? Why encumber

him with forerunners at all?

rod smith

Bugs, they put these bennies in the liver
to make us not so human on their inconsistent curves
placed hips that turn left into worry
committees of people designed to collectively swerve

it's lonely here up in Virginia
yet I want to be one of those people
who dip into it when needed
bird over center meridian
bringing down double-sad Roma song for you

see, abuse the legions
and the Romans will care more about you
regiments of children pushing faces up to grass
it's a full-time business, being Sulu next to someone
being someone alone at the curve by the deer in the fog

then, at the border, where the singers come to find you
the future can be swallowed and more easily borne inside
just picture all the sunspots on the livers of the pious
their secret ingestible whiskeyfied cruciform light

when it goes, they will write poems to us
because we have broken each snifter of glass in their bar
singly and with great deliberation
"now you've got nothing to worry 'bout any no more"

Labor Day

So I say to my friend at the day job
"We are bored sometimes, and scented like realtors
but if everyone's equally disconsolate
under labor's gooey caul
then nuance can be stitched more vividly
to secrets lodged inside of everyone
until it becomes your own country
with highways that carry you silently past the jetty
which, from their heavy drinking, the case managers come out to
failing to be stable and badly attempting to sing"

We're pushing our barques past the mansions
as I say this, near the dwellings of persons
whose lives have no mooring
outside the slow fact of our passing—
huddled arrogantly under their air-conditioning
they want us to be users
moved by advertisers
enticing the constituency
to join them and sit there and weep

But we're too busy pulling
toward centers where workers assemble.
While time for them is a melody
played at long intervals across condominiums

we who are the power

know our systems so much better

now come to this hour outside it

now give it new form on guitar

Larry's House of Brakes

Consider the interiors at Larry's House of Brakes
or study the sensible physics of drag & baffle;
there is no valid manual on stopping.
And while feelings can rarely be described or even discerned
with any real exactitude by anyone,
the fact of their motion is constant and perceptible.
Even with institutions as chilly and indifferent as the stars,
whose permutations resemble episodes in the later seasons
of a once-popular sitcom, where everyone has ended up with everyone
else, the plot slackens, the characters don't evolve
and things get absurdly mystical,
you still sense in the mere rotation
a heroic and enormous effort to nudge the myth forward
despite all arguments against velocity
or bruised elbows or the danger of burning on fire escapes
which is also a fairly good analogue for probably what we are,
or I am, in the long stretches where I'm not sure when
we'll be together, and time gets all Sadducee and evil
refusing to accelerate while knowing what I want
is just four of your hours, or a shared plate of spaghetti
or you sitting near me at a poetry reading or someplace
equally public, forgetting to despise me just a little.

La Chevy Nova

One of the great pivots in Christian history
occurs near the end of canto 27 of Dante's *Purgatorio*, a
canto that opens with the pilgrim comparing the dying sky
to Christ's vermilion wounds (note the "sun"
deftly figured here as "son") and the Ebro
and the Ganges, which are rivers,
are empurpled—made royal—by noon
and a glad angel shows up to sing gladly
about the flame that will burn but also purifies,
which our pilgrim by the end of the canto will have to go through
like the muscles behind or just on top of the knee can burn
at the end of a long run, or perhaps (and here's the pivot)
like the burning some do when they go from a car
at night's end in a remote parking lot
where nothing is unseemly or sordid
but does in a fashion burn, but also does it purify
as history considered in its Christian dimension must also purify?

Dante, you'll remember, has spent the preceding cantiche
skillfully working his personal crotchets
into a gargantuan cosmic structure—"I vividly recalled
the human bodies I had once seen burned"—
with his obduracy not once being softened;
yet he manages to nest this ugly effort
in the larger project of turning his passion for the dead Beatrice
into a redemptive program for himself, for time, the reeling stars,

the fishes, the beestes, the air and everything in it
and finally, one might point out, for movement itself
which is seen at the end from its center and revealed as an aspect of love.

Structure is on fire, and tercets are on fire, and process
is on fire, and motion is on fire; while the poem has learned
to preen and turn, pivot on itself, and no longer hurts, or points
at a world, or even at its status as an internally consistent
verbal object, only at the most tiresome conditions
of its own production.
                              But I gaze at you and I burn
with a new vernacular; I see you and I see vermilion,
your color—vermilion in the stoplights
and the stoplights ranged as stars
like the stars could spell out B-E-A-T-R-I-C-E
and would if they weren't so dim and talky, stuck
in their orbits where it's safe to promise love—"it
hurts, but you won't die"—and you stew in a tepid
amor amicitiae, Socrates spooning
with Alicibiades, warm under sheets
against philosophy's cold stars:
"It hurts, but you won't die."

That even a wound, even now, could make things pure
is enough to count me bitten,
returned to the pivoting folds of this world:
count me hurt, count me bitten.
Gulls distribute themselves over Oakland's industrial center
like I leave you, come back to be near you

where I hear their glad song, or watch them scatter gladly

over the beautiful chords of this world;

and beautiful are the chords of this world

with you and everything in it;

beautiful the Ebro above the phone lines

emitting its fine vermilion into morning

so pleasing to mine and to everybody's eyes.

So do I live to look at you and so

does everyone: It hurts, but I won't die—

a little sun, a little wound

"but through that little space I saw the stars."

The Leftenant

On maps it would appear as the size of a chestnut—

it would fit inside a ventricle—

but there is no room for maps

and nothing would prepare you for the journey

to learn about the children

individually ruined inside it

yet exactly in the same way every time

so that you could display it like anapests

powerfully burned into windows

for dismemberment to read and choose among.

Was this a country? They do not talk,

but seem to come alive for the poet.

So really there are two countries:

one is the district seen from a divan,

the other was the government that came into my heart

showily but without embarrassment,

protecting aspects of my service

laminated in a wallet

dropped casually somewhere inside the embassy.

When I got back

I noticed of the people who were angry,

there were angry people moved by what they didn't believe

angry for years, but without messages

and it seemed wrong to spill out

a whole burden of aesthetics

while life continues moving for them

fast as commercials in Spanish,

nativizing product into ghost.

Are they listening to someone

outside the warm enclosure of the poem

among the disassembled furnishings

of the country I was in,

a lamp at a vigil

swinging on a pole

and then, below the windows,

me putting all these colors in a box?

gary sullivan

Thousands of users are assigning stars
to illumine the people

we find or know,
tapirs asleep in the verdure

of Belize, just shriveled up in wilderness
like that. I wanted to show you

its birthday cake
but gots to maintain that dental hygiene, right?

The adventure is dead,
there are newer adventures

and if all we are really passionate for is just
to meet, then reach out to your fandom

via science, go use that science background
as part of the earlier trilogy

connecting the books to true life.
A trip to the e-mail, a grand electric calm—

I've read the generations
reach sexual maturity faster

testing all the software
nobody slowly reads.

The colorful detritus of information
gathers, comes to rest

amid the tiny spaces of the capital.
The adventure isn't over,

tapirs in the verdure
days when you could just be on top of a pyramid

via fibers bearing sleep—
the adventure's not dead

but who will keep the genre?
Because at least part of it happened

I turn a little Oscar for you
here, on a lathe

And I love it, it's what got me into the adventure genre.
And I love it, it's what got me into the adventure genre.

At the Small Bar in the Embassy

Here's what I said to the desert

when I met it, spruced up and matched with amazing wines

at the small bar in the embassy. A handful of guests had already arrived

and suddenly I wanted to be writing

something about the insides of metal detectors,

about how the desert used to be a river

and wine sloshed against Mars's canals once like surf

in its youth, which was our youth

but we never think to ask it

when the desert is here, with us at the bar,

about its wild era, only after the foie gras has come,

the ambassador's wife gone upstairs with a slim apparatchik

and machines that blow snow

have exhausted themselves

on the desert, which has no other place to go

apparently when you are a desert you are always at home

you are home even here

at this bar

home with machines blowing snow

slow poem

slow things heard in old songs

sad songs sung by the sides of old inns

dry roses clutched by a lover

a wedding dress downriver

you will ask them their names

the women who remember

will ask you in turn where you come from

inside this small country

you are writing a book

it's unfinished

the evening enfolding you slowly

a soreness in the fingers

who are you they ask

you will get in the car

with the mirror with the silver

flaking in the back

the book will receive much criticism

you knew it from the story

the bride gone downriver

where dusk pulls the sunset

quarter after quarter

so many have written

they will ask you in roses

will ask what to call you

by the river where you come

epithalamion

the silence, the season

the centaurs returning

a day for the razors,

the Lapiths in cups

women, the moon

the centaurs with daggers:

turn back from our women,

turn back to the wood

beasts on the friezes

eternally turning

moon on the temple

o women, return

slavoj žižek

suffer the children

to come to my Myspace

get out of the kitchen or I'm having a divorce

the war as it was happening in a lot of my classes

Internet's power versus today's multiculturalism

Slavoj Žižek all the trees have bloomed

spreading because of my hair weave on YouTube

it wasn't that I wanted it particularly

she'd just walk and it would fall off like that

Looking back at the Etruscans

it must have been cloudy

moon in a bucket and friends across the Alps

your work too seems to have this distance

U.N. instructors in the valleys of Slovenia

teaching remedial high school boys guitar

my life in the nineties

is funding the problem

of gothic freshmen stupefied on amps

Sorry I'm temporarily unavailable

except from this spot in the kitchen I get two bars

Žižek, Slavoj (b. 1949)

American pioneer women

made Quonsets from Leviticus

concessionaires in rings around New York

Goodbye Slavoj Žižek

I should probably finish *Comus*

box of collected Olympic apparel pins

My wife and I are parents

of a beautiful daughter from China

why can't a common language foster peace

Jazz Impressions
of Gazprom

Labor scab, you owe me
for the drinks drunk in Hawaii
that we gave the apparatchiks
   to string management from trees

Each new time I punch you
a fissure sends a gas plume
above the Czech Republic
   where the ladies love my ghee

It's just business—gluing shtetls
to excuses for the awnings
stuck with numbers of suppliers
   with their music on CD

Surfers, hear me check statistics
like a lover come downriver
past the estuary pipeworks
   through night's orthopedic sleeve

Put a man inside a tanker
and he'll treat you like a Habsburg
being martyred at a border
   to consolidate the see

It's so lonesome here, Monsignor
but they block my work computer
you will find the best chorizo
    under domes the churchly flee

Come and crowd my cramped bodega
Ms. Provocatrix in pantsuit,
I've abandoned economics
    so cassette for you is free

I can orchestrate your folk dance,
little Hussite with a handbag,
cap the oil with a nipple
    and the line stops killing bream

Lara, I'm so spattered
with your theme inside the movie
that's your ring down in my cocktail?
    I'm pure green boy energy

In the dark, I do my thinking
if the movie has an ending
if it doesn't, hear me breathing
    on your fake neuropathy

You're no good at being viscous,
I looked younger in Peshawar.
She is foreign, with a seester?
    I am coming. Let me be.

For the Assorted (Vulcan Love Song)

You always are the assorted within my arms
one tastes repellent, Choose another
Today I am being the center of the universe:
You were always the last to remain
Man, you crack me up, Michelle
"Always Still on the Slavery"*

You who are always the assorted in my arms
Who knows what the hell this song means?
. . . they were high . . .
he saw some chick backlit and the sun
going through her he thought
"*It's not a world, they're initials*," meaning

Today I am repellent inside your arms
The chunks in the cheese
all backlit, unassorted and disarmed
the sun being neglected
while hearing this poem on the radio
man, are you still on the slavery?

Even the Vulcans, in their cool federations
might warm to be cream in your arms
because they were high but their words also kinda
make sense. . . . you were always the last
of the slaves to initial "*today we'll be better*
o center of earth between arms"

Poem

I've been wanting to write you in the open, gorgeous manner of Frank
   O'Hara
but the hegemony of the everyday gets in the way
and fucks with my insouciance—how to be chatty or bright
as a dime when you feel like the vaguely urinous taste in the morning
   coffee
they serve at the Golden Donuts behind the office park
I work in, where the owner and I routinely discuss our children
and I feel sort of proud but also so old,
like a rotary phone that won't let you connect to a voicemail system
that's newer, and probably also blacks the ear like Kenneth
Koch's in O'Hara's great poem "Poem"
beginning with the line: "The fluorescent tubing burns like a bobby-
soxer's ankles," which he wrote when he was only 33
and I'm 36, and you're 25
for one more week, and you, too, maybe will soon be crying
De pro-fund-is clamavi over the sparrowy death of your youth
which doesn't so much die

As simply lose the reassuring quality it once possessed, like gravity,
and begins to present itself more like a question: "Are we just muddy
   instants"
in the larger Irrawaddy of process? Or excuses for Hermes
to pull trick coins from the vague and unused space behind our eyes?
   Obscurely we know

we are all slowly dying—I maybe of drinking (though the halcyon days
    of dying
of drink are over), you of a surfeit of something, probably pleasure,
which cloys over time because of the way desires have
of behaving like carnival ducks under neon tubing
that we suffer to be shot at again and again, until after a while you begin
    to lose faith
in the effectiveness of the whole procedure
which involves setting them back up and pretending it's different ducks
moving in a firm line across the horizon, under new lighting,
instead of the same ones wearily describing the same occluded circle.

I'm not convinced there's anything in what I'm saying
you couldn't find equally well in O'Hara, or *Conversations*
with Eckermann, or Robert Musil: but "great ideas that command
instant allegiance" are hard to find, if they even exist, which leaves the
    lesser ones
without much to do except vie for our temporary affections
and those can settle almost anywhere, like birds freight a phone line
or sunburns exult at a summer beach resort. Still, there's some quality
in our peculiar allegiance this completely passes over,
and while the thought of you as merely a great idea is as difficult to
    imagine
as a sex offender staying chaste on Google,
the part about the instant makes some sense—
things happen with us at such wicked speeds, but over such a small
    surface
that velocity itself becomes an aspect of feeling,

suggestive of the chaos and rich sense of purpose

that arrives with the beginning of any new century, where everything for

a short time

seems to stretch over something larger and younger and sweeter than

itself

and no detail is too trivial to contain it, or at least point to its imminent

disclosure

in a future full of passionate enjoyment

that we all know must be coming because the detail itself is with us

here, in the present, managing to reflect it

by sitting there just winking and being a part of its time.

I guess it's possible for any one of us to say with Goethe:

"I should have been happier, and should have accomplished more as

a poet";

but saying it next to you it sounds faintly ridiculous,

exuding the cedary odor of attempts by sterner ages

to press all the lovely, redolent fragments thrown out

with its neckerchiefs or cabriolets up against one another

until they formed a whole. Whether their effort was really so different

from our own wish for freeway diners that stay "Always Open"

or an America detached from the systems that squeak to produce it

is one of those questions we so casually leave to History

like a mismatched sock or an outdated computer monitor

while pursuing "This her free hand in my own

demanding presence," an activity which the present seems so ardently

to insist upon, like aging, though the trick is in learning

how to release it, and let things just sort of meander

until they uncover their own demands

as if the time they took to unfold in was itself a kind of poem

that manages in its last crushing stanza

to intimate mortality and its shivery sense of importance

While talking about ephemera

like bobby-soxers or neon tubing

without ever saying why it is they finally age, or burn,

just putting them there, in the poem,

incomplete and beautiful like you.

marianne moore

In her lifetime, she was as much noted

for being an eccentric

as for letting her presbyterian mother steelily over-revise.

Her public life attracted many readers

while moments that were private

remained conflicted and abstract.

Though celebrity entices many

into the ramparts abutting the harbor,

just cruise for a minute the world

of poetry and already you have shaped it.

Critics point and point to define a vision

where reality falls short—

what Moore did was she wrote and wrote

a poetry inside her life,

speaking directly (she did not need philosophies)

to the subtle confusions of time.

She did this without any philosophy;

instead, poetry asked her, "What is *life*?"

Though it went through some revisions

multiplicity in her life had several urges

that felt for the sun like tendrils

against the dark weight of the author's times.

Each stage of life

is reflected in new changes to her poems

so that writing can suggest a slow precession

away from how the world is not to be.

Most critics address just merits; do they think

of how the world is not to be?

Whatever Moore was writing,

she adopted the tricornered hat.

That's fame, in all its pretension

and sometimes it stretches backward to blacken whole lives.

One version shouldn't be considered worse or better,

because why is it completion can't reside

in a poem just as finely as the corners of a hat?

What is it that keeps the beauty and the life

forever considered in the abstract separately?

Most critics preen like vendors;

my goal here is to juggle containers

until no single kind of poetry speaks better

or is even more important than any other

and we're forced to consider something

that is whole. Later I will consider

why there are so many critics of this poem

and guide the community gently to revise it.

I will abandon the misguided steps

of adjuncts who summon reality only when it's popular

and ask why the tricornered hat

was lost to fashion

especially given its role in the early struggles

exhibited in most of the contours of Moore's life.

Put what she attempts to accomplish

on a trencher beside what she thought poetry should be,

then what she said to readers

in an urn that holds and concentrates

whatever she still conveys to us today.

Does one resist the falls of life,

the other make a padding for the barrel?

Or do both provide a yellow haze

for obscuring the different stunts of poetry?

Withdrawn for a period,

then after, much more outward with her writing

a fox hauling grapes from its covert

to place against depression and war and war.

It made the poems more accessible,

how her life informed each new variation

making it simpler for recent fans

to cringe and progress through the age.

Though what was it with her life that she was saying?

And was it even legible to her?

Death has a profound effect

on contemplations of what makes life important.

It's visible as everything you've written, but only after,

so that what Moore tends to say about writing

breaks down into tragic divisions

that propel new kinds of distinctions

mixing strict morals

with a powerful verse message for today.

Think how her affections

are like changes to an emblem

on a gonfalon of fabric

that is variegated, precious, and immense;

Then think how we all trail it

drawing a list together

of every poem ever made in English

and putting her maybe permanently on it

which reveals me I guess as a critic

wheeling my small history

behind me from conference to conference

discussing Moore's advances to sensation

sense of fashion life revision

struggles mothers tendrils critics

god death hats toads fame

Traditional Countertops

I sometimes feel held back by you socially

because we are from such different traditions

of things you shouldn't eat

Yet, being poor, we are ready to suffer

death as it conventionally arrives in poems

a celebrity fragrance

promising rest from statistics

not looking at you directly

but knowing each island that touches you socially

in echo and sweat under skin

First at a villa, then in a district

whose windows opened out

onto social planes I can no longer see,

properties with neighboring villas

whose neighbors sit so close so as not to face you

quietly in their traditions, under their creations

alphabetic and shiny

their countertops around you all the time

Flanking you socially—economic digitalis

agents of the episteme of marble

recurring on these islands over time

Lands your fathers came from

out to meet you, meet your looking

imagine them seeing you now,

inside this city

among these absorbent countertops

their white, traditional countertops

you stain them if you eat

You Are Dreaming the Wrong Dream

I have a friend

who awakened a dream

but ground it into different kinds of dreamers.

What strikes me most forcibly

is how I was a kind friend

but also the dream

unlived and pushing out its waves

into new brands of dreamers

who were some of them my friends

but some in a business group

and some the root problem

that kept the others working

on a beautiful pink temple

straddling the perimeter

of everyone else's dream

made with many people from the town.

Let's not worry about it now,

but I woke with that truth

carrying its bricks up my long summit

participating in filling a swampy ground

over bigger sorts of problems

until you had to be a specialist in something

for dreaming to even take notice

of your building and your sleeping on that ground.

Because in the end it must all be dismantled,
shedding crimson stamens in the springtime
then waking from the middle of my life
following the echo down the temple
to others who still love me
the dreaming and its dreamer
pulled into competing wings

For you to touch together
atop the weedy breastworks
housing the indigenes
who just hug you when you visit
in their hutment on the commons
my base of love poured even
more securely over that.

I know a friend
who livens up group thinking
by building an enclosure
out of other people's difference—
people painting on the temple
some are digging out the foyers
others writing on the narthex
and I encourage you to read them
and I hope you check out their dream.

jack spicer

That's autumn, purple in his tresses
Totally cloying.
No one likens potters to their ochre,
Dun hoppers for meats to be live in. Drop a
Character in water, it means
Nothing.
I
Am dyed and paired with buyers
Like a paint. The drab
Nouns men pound hoops for. Angular
Ponces on a shore. Beat with less signal. No
Poem's green as it ought to be.

nocturne

Across the news, the moon

to feed the hungry?

or trace silver cantos

in dark collegiate forecourts.

Its deeds are so minimal

by map it's still night

rich and lustrous and poor enough

for America's urban and suburban areas to shine into,

a satellite for motto

phone number of the inventor of the lyric

possibly Ambrel's party photo pics

a rite or custom brings us each together

to prefer or to be judged by non-applause.

no title

after all the usual modes of adoption
you trade lives with the diocese
now there is courage and now there is loss
new space for the brethren's exhaling
re-breathed into you

a spur of foam
that empties into reverence
there is bread there and broth
a confusion of rooms

the dawn road from the capital
past misused industries
you at different times adopted

pity the convoy that goes down it
carrying tears and carrying names
one brake in a field of breathings
it is gone

Bardic Genetics

This poem is essentially about life and death.

What is clear about this particular poem, compared to most poetry,

is that through the voice of the speaker the reader can feel the

    emotions and thoughts of the author

flattening down into points

that come across as very personal

to delight and sadden the younger readers of today.

In almost all other poetry there is a "speaker"

who goes upward and upward,

a machine that absorbs vibration from bigger machines

but if it happens here now, in this poem

will there be anyone nearby who wants to see?

Maybe the dead know how to live more fully,

torches turned down but still fuming

like rinds around hot marshmallows do,

their divided subject matter focused primarily

on dark imagery with symbols of light inside——

I never understood the big whoop about Demeter:

reading is already a giant supplanting.

A new reader discovers this work

while he is leaving flowers where his dead bride used to be.

But it enables him to be reborn again each time——

Persephone is not the unhappy one

    moving up the dark stairs

she considers in her consciousness as light

while the poem commences and commences

like the days dividing summer from its students,

sponges that sway in an undersea film

Until the poem spreads, and reaches its conclusion

that students are each taught to believe in things differently:

that Persephone was a goddess

who was abducted by Pluto,

the author himself a blue web that exists

years and years after his death

stuck inside the tired envelope of poetry

Who feels he finally is reading himself,

the spring flowers intense and papery

like they used to be, enabling the reader

again to feel the darkness

with a rhythm that enables the reader to almost see.

Was his conclusion merely a mistake, or did he intentionally

use elements of different poems until he finally made

his destination, from blue to smoking to flatten,

September confused with its light?

Etruria

The Kingdom of Etruria was Napoleon's contrivance;

it existed at his pleasure, baroque, ephemeral.

To get girls who don't normally drink whiskey to drink

requires some contrivance. Plot is often dismissed

as a contrivance—even pornos have them—but try

negotiating time without one. Thrones

provoke pretenders, kingship suffers kings.

The larger point lurking behind this is that all

art is contrivance, not just the classy result

of thought. A drunk scene here, a drunk scene there,

more thought. For me, it's more of a conveyance;

you can jiggle it all you want, but it still dispenses the authentic

like water bottles to exhausted marathon runners

thirsty from their forward trudge through time.

Nothing is truly connected, if art is Truth. There is no real

analogy between being "high" on LSD and "drunk" on whiskey;

the postage stamp carries no stain of the eminence it represents.

Bourbon is county, booze, and kings

and admittedly there's some room for awkward slippage here;

Hermes honeys tongues of poets and thieves indiscriminately,

which nudges us toward the question of art being hermetic,

a matter of discriminations, exclusion's game face.

Let's contrive to avoid this issue—quicklime

to any discussion—and forge ahead to Napoleon.

His improvised kingdom: politics or art?

Aestheticizing politics was a hallmark of the Fascists,

but politicizing aesthetics remains a valid practice for the Left.

There's one of those slippages again, they crop up

like Bourbons, so many pretenders to an illusory throne.

A rich sense of the ironic comes in handy

if you're a World Historical Figure; then, when History

bends back on itself, or strays "off topic" in the manner

of schoolboys in classrooms with too many windows,

you're ready to pretend there's still something like significance

in the gap between the temporal and the meaningful

so many human events seem to happen in,

filling like a sluice cleverly contrived to contain them

in which the philosophical or merely powerful

contrive to read a goodness and fullness and purpose

few of the rest of us perceive. They try to make artists

look loony, though why? Crowning yourself a Napoleon

makes waves in certain circles, but the claim goes frankly

unacknowledged pretty much everywhere else.

Still, if language is the gendarmery of thought,

what does that say about thinking? Gendarmes?

Popes are primates, primates apes; before the world wars plunged everybody

into catastrophe, how many gave thought to the strangeness in that?

Maybe Napoleon, who made his name in the desert

only to lose it to a dessert. Now poesy and its purpose

contrive to change every few years, the proverbial snake

shedding its proverbial skin into the various anthologies bent to receive it

until the whole idea of innovation and the author who suffers

to produce it starts to seem a little, well, contrived.

Wars get forgotten and are replaced with new ones,

disaster is palimpsest to modernity's radiant texts.

Then we became precipitations of our speech acts,

extensions of form, Etrurian courtiers fanning the phenomenal

with the soul's broad palms, whose fiats

and pronunciamentos got so shrill and boring

in its last sick years, before we contrived to invert its astonishing structure

and put the nose back squarely before the Sphinx. Now everyone's

relatively happy, with lots of theoretically interesting things to say about

just about everything. Capitals evoke letters and cities,

theaters are redolent of pretense and of wars.

I think we're more comfortable with not always being rational

despite the unsettling sense that Reason is on the march somewhere

like History and Progress and Science and Time

advancing on the Bourbons of Etruria,

drunk drunk drunk drunk drunk drunk drunk.

Acknowledgments

Grateful acknowledgments are made to the editors and friends at the following publications, in which many of these poems first appeared:

Abraham Lincoln: "Etruria," "Indignant Puppies," "sharon mesmer,"
"slavoj žižek," "Tiny Spark"

Aufgabe: "ghazal," "no title"

BOTH BOTH: "Googly World," "I Am Sitting in a Room," "jack spicer,"
"Traditional Countertops," "You Are Dreaming the Wrong Dream"

Canteen: "Occitan Reverb," "The Women Are Weaning at the Cutter
of the Now"

Dusie: "For the Assorted (Vulcan Love Song)"

Fourteen Hills: "Billet-don't"

MiPOesias: "Tristia"

The Nation: "slow poem"

Parthenon West Review: "La Chevy Nova," "The Real Aeneid"

Peaches and Bats: "Bardic Genetics," "The Leftenant"

Portland Review: "valerie bertinelli"

Saginaw: "nichita stănescu," "Pyjamas"

Shampoo: "Happy Xmas," "Jazz Impressions of Gazprom"

The Tiny: "Community Sing"

Try!: "At the Small Bar in the Embassy," "jack spicer," "Labor Day,"
"Noises for the Talkies"

Viz. Inter-Arts: "Poem"

West Wind Review: "marianne moore," "rod smith"

Work: "chinoiserie," "epithalamion," "gary sullivan," "nocturne"

Xantippe: "Larry's House of Brakes"

ZYZZYVA: "Toward a Theory of Translation"

Earlier versions of some of these poems appeared in the chapbook *Rules for Drinking Forties* (Cy Press, 2009), published by Dana Ward. Thank you, Dana. "At the Small Bar in the Embassy" was printed as a coaster broadside for Small Press Traffic by Cuneiform Press in 2011.

A special thanks to K. Silem Mohammad, Julian Talamantez Brolaski, Cynthia Sailers, David Brazil, Alli Warren, Brandon Brown, David Larsen, Brent Cunningham, the Flarflist Collective, and the Wave team (Joshua Beckman on first) for lights in the dark.